The Ultimate Monologue Book
for Middle School Actors Volume IV

111 One-Minute Monologues
The Rich, The Famous, The Historical

A Smith and Kraus Book
Published by Smith and Kraus, Inc.
177 Lyme Road, Hanover, NH 03755
www.smithandkraus.com

© 2008 by Kristen Dabrowski
All rights reserved.

LIMITED REPRODUCTION PERMISSION:
The publisher grants permission to individual teachers
to reproduce the scripts as needed for use with their own students.
Permission for reproduction for an entire school district
or for commercial use is required. Please call Smith and Kraus, Inc.
at (603) 643-6431, fax (603) 643-1831.

First Edition: February 2008
Manufactured in the United States of America
10 9 8 7 6 5 4 3 2 1

Cover and text design by Julia Gignoux, Freedom Hill Design

ISBN: 978-1-57525-579-8
Library of Congress Control Number: 2007942602

The Ultimate Monologue Book for Middle School Actors
VOLUME IV
• • •
111 One-Minute Monologues
The Rich, The Famous The Historical

Kristen Dabrowski

YOUNG ACTORS SERIES

Smith and Kraus, Inc.
Hanover, New Hampshire

DEDICATION

To Amy and Mom for their encouragement.
To Mr. Dabrowski for being my educational consultant.
To Kate and Julia for bringing everything together.

CONTENTS

Introduction ix
Teacher's Guide xi

Animated, Mythical, and Biblical Figures. 1
Answers. 14

Icons of Literature, Art, and Fashion 15
Answers. 38

Stars of TV, Film, and Music 39
Answers. 54

World Leaders 55
Answers. 74

Revolutionaries and Innovators 75
Answers. 86

Athletes and Adventurers. 87
Answers. 98

Presidents, Vice Presidents, and First Ladies. 99
Answers. 108

Scientists, Inventors, Doctors, and Nurses 109
Answers. 122

Spies, Informers, Reporters,
   Newsmakers, and Money Takers 123
Answers. 134

   Index of Names. 135

   The Author 137

Introduction

Hello, actors! As a professional actor for fourteen years now, I know how hard the search for the perfect monologue can be. To make the search more fun, this book contains two twists: (1) the characters are based on famous people and (2) you have to guess who's who! You may discover some information about a famous or historical person you never knew before. Some monologues are based on real events; other monologues are entirely fanciful and imaginary. The dialogue contains clues that will help. Read them carefully! Try testing your friends, your parents, and your teachers. Answers are in the back of each section.

Though these monologues are based on notable figures, the situations are relatable to kids and teens today. It's important to remember that even famous people who lived hundreds of years ago were real and had real problems. (The same is true for fictional characters! They echo real people's lives as well.) Be sure, when you are reading and performing these monologues, that you make the characters seem like real people.

Here are some tips on approaching monologues:

1. Pick the monologue that hits you. Trust your instincts. You'll pick the right one!

2. Make the monologues active. What do you want and how do you try to get it?

3. Who are you talking to and where is he or she? Make sure you make this as clear as possible.

4. Do you get answered or interrupted? Be sure to fill in words in your head for the moments when you are spoken to in the monologue, even if it's a simple yes or no.

5. How do you feel about the person or people you are talking to? For example, you speak a lot differently to your best friend than you do to your math teacher.

- **Résumé/Your Turn:** Once students understand the premise behind this book, compile a list of additional illustrious figures (for example, Howard Hughes, Warren Buffet, Mark Twain, Queen Victoria, Madonna). Each student will pick a name from the list (or from a hat). Hand out a résumé form for students to fill out about their character, which includes the following topics: Employment Ambition, Family Background, Early Work Experience, Greatest Achievements, Strong Personality Traits, References. After completing the résumé form, students will write monologues about their chosen figure at a young age. From here, students' work can be used in any of the other activities listed here.

- **Acting Day:** Have students work on the monologues in class. Choose a day where they perform their memorized and rehearsed monologue. To add difficulty, have students dress and act like their character throughout class.

- **True or Imagined Challenge:** Read the monologues and discuss what's true and what's imagined. What inferences have been made about the famous or historical figures? Do students agree or disagree with the assessment? Is anything historically inaccurate? Can they relate to the character?

- **Connect Four:** Present groups with four monologues based on historical characters. Have the group discuss what life circumstances the historical figures have in common (such as having to leave school, living in poverty, experiencing racism, having distant parents, being wealthy). How did their experiences contribute to who they became? How does adversity shape a person's life? This exercise can segue easily into the following one.

- **Believe/Me:** Create a handout with a few key questions about personal beliefs. Here are a few examples: Do you believe in God? Would you rather be a parent of three kids or the owner of three pets? Which is more important—money, popularity, or inner peace? Do you prefer big parties or a quiet night with friends? Discuss together or in groups what these answers might signal about students' futures. Are they more likely to be a doctor or a revolutionary? A business whiz or an army general? A florist or a politician? From here, have students look at monologues and see which one they relate to most. Discuss why they feel the character they chose is most like them.

- **Looks Can Be Deceiving/A Picture Is Worth a Thousand Words:** Print out pictures of the monologue characters and have students match the pictures to the monologues. See if students can go through their reasoning. Are looks deceiving or is a picture worth a thousand words? For example, when he was twelve, did anyone guess that Bill Gates would be the billionaire entrepreneur he is today? Looking at Mae West, does her photo scream "sexy movie star"? This can be opened up into discussions about ethics, identity, and behavior. Everyone is a real person with real issues as an adolescent; you never know who will be rich, powerful, or influential as an adult. As a follow-up project, give students a picture of a person you haven't studied yet and have them write a monologue about what they think this person was like when he or she was younger.

- **Shuffle:** Give each student a monologue. Do not tell them their character's name. Based on their monologue, have the students break into cliques. Which other people (based on the monologue alone) would their character like? Now let the students know the name of their character. Tape up on the walls some chapter headings (like the ones in this book). Then have the students determine in which chapter their monologue should go. Many characters can go into more than one chapter! Are the people in your chapter the same people that were in your clique? Why or why not? Lastly, have students break into chronological groups. (This might take a little research!) For example, everyone born in the 1800s would stand together. Then see and discuss which people from the other groups (the clique and the chapter) are still present. What do the people in this group have in common? Have people changed over time or are there certain issues or personality types that always exist? (Note: There are many variations on this game. You can try breaking into groups based on birth country, race, or education level, which can begin some very interesting discussions. Ask students how these factors influenced their character's life, personality, or decisions, if at all.)

If you like what you see, check out the other seventeen books I've written. In particular, the *10+* play series has short plays, scenes, and monologues with performance tips, writing ideas, discussion questions after each play, and several games and exploration activities. As always, you are invited to give me comments and ideas at monologuemadness@yahoo.com.

Enjoy!

Kristen Dabrowski

Animated, Mythical, and Biblical Figures

• • •

Mr. Clean

Burger King

Santa Claus

Fat Albert

Delilah

Hades

Medea

Peter Parker

The Tooth Fairy

Dairy Queen

Persephone

SWEET

Go on. Have ice cream for dinner. And breakfast. And lunch! You know you want to. All the cool kids are doing it. Come on. No one's here but you and me. Who will know?

Who am I? *(Fill in the blank with the correct character)*, of course! Don't forget chocolate sauce. And whipped cream. Mmm-mmmm!

I am not gaining a few pounds! Besides, a little cushioning is healthy. Otherwise, it hurts to sit down. Have some crushed up Oreos on that.

Plus, this outfit isn't so flattering, so it's not fair to judge my appearance. I have to dress like a German five-year-old. I can't believe anyone chooses to wear clogs. They're uncomfortable. Cherries. You need cherries. Food and people can never be too sweet!

You're a cutie. Wanna go out sometime for a hot fudge brownie sundae? With mint chocolate chip ice cream and caramel topping, of course.

BAKING

One day my dad tells me to go to my room. So I do, because he's basically the most powerful guy in the universe. Next thing I know, I'm here in this world of eternal darkness, just me and my two little devil dogs, the Hounds of Hell. Sounds like a great name for a rock group, don't it? Man, I could go for a Twinkie. I don't have those down here. There's no baking in hell.

I really dug this Persephone chick, but she's not into me because she says I'm scary. People are so judgmental. I just look Goth because I was brought up this way. When you're in the depths of the Underworld, you can't really keep up-to-date with trends. Someone actually told me that metal is dead. That people listen to guys singing really high, and sometimes those same guys are wearing braids??? What is going on up there? When I was alive, little girls sang high and wore braids.

And all I hear all day from you babies is how unfair everything is for you. My father sent me to the Underworld. FOREVER! What did your dad do? Tell you to finish your homework? Please. Get back to me when you have some real problems. And next time you come, bring chocolate chip cookies.

BIG AND PROUD

My name is *(fill in the blank with the correct character)*. Not—what did you call me?—Bees? Why do you keep calling me that? I don't even know what that means. Oh—bees. That's not my name; don't call me that!

No, it doesn't bother me being fat. So what? No one bothers me. Except you. Everyone else likes my jokes and thinks I'm a lot of fun. No one makes fun of me 'cause I could flatten them. Being fat is cool. Does it bother you that you're skinny?

Well, then, shut your mouth and mind your own business.

DESTINY

Mom and Dad, am I adopted? How come I'm so much bigger than my brothers? I know I eat more sweets, but—I'm taller, too. Yeah, I know I'm special. If I've got a special mission in life, don't you think it's about time you tell me about it? I'm tired of all the secrets. I'm old enough now. Tell me the truth.

Wait a minute. Do I have a choice? I always wanted to be a baseball player and move to Florida. Can I do that instead? No? Are you serious? What do I get out of it?

I'm going to travel the world? And give stuff away? So what. What do I care about little kids everywhere? What did they ever do for me?

I get all the candy and chocolate I want? Well, OK. If I have to.

JOB HAZARDS

Ew, ew, ew, ew, ew! I'm never going to get used to this. This job is gross. No kidding. Oh, sure, it's fun for the kid who finds money, but for me? Think about it. I'm touching something that's been in someone's mouth. Who knows whether it's been cleaned off?

Now this kid, he's a deep sleeper. But there are loads of kids who wake up if you breathe on them. And if you wake someone up, there's a huge amount of magic you have to do to make things right again.

Don't let anyone fool you. Being *(fill in the blank with the correct character)* is not all fun and games!

ARACHNIPHOBIA

Ah! Oh my God! Kill it, kill it, kill it! I just hate bugs! I know they're smaller than me, but there's just something about bugs that creeps me out. I just have to jump back.

I'm not a sissy! Do you like bugs? Really like them? Come on, no one really likes bugs. They're gross—crawling on your skin, lots of legs all sticky and creepy-crawly! Everyone pretends not to be bothered by them, but it's instinct to want to get away from them. Don't you think there might be a reason for it? Maybe we're scared for a reason. Like some people don't like sharks or ghosts. Maybe it's because they're going to be eaten by a shark or haunted by a ghost!

It's not stupid! OK, fine. I'll kill that spider. Just give me a minute.

I RULE

I am your leader! Bow down! I am *(fill in the blank with the correct character)*. Let there be grease! Let them have apple pie with no apples in it and eat it too! Peasants, slaves, serfs, get me a Coke so large I can put my feet in it. Didn't you hear me? Do it now before I condemn you to garbage duty and the tyranny of the deep fryer.

You can't overthrow me. My name is on the sign.

There will be no democracy. You will toil forever under me.

I have a proclamation! "*(Fill in the blank with the correct character)* makes no claim that there will be actual meat in the burgers, nor does he claim there will be no meat in the veggie burgers!" The king has spoken! Have a nice day!

OBSESSIVE

Ahhh! Mom! Something terrible is happening to me! Yesterday, when I was cleaning the house from top to bottom, I got dizzy from the ammonia fumes. Next thing I knew, I woke up with my head in a bucket! Ever since then, my hair has been falling out! I love it when the house is spic and span, but am I taking my cleanliness too far?

You're right. It's probably my tight pants cutting off the circulation to my head. What could be better than a house that sparkles? Gotta go! I think I heard some dust fall on the toilet!

MY QUEST

Jason is handsome, isn't he? And he's strong. The moment I saw him . . . Well, he's perfect. Do you think he likes me? He asked me to help him with some tasks he has to do. That's a good sign, isn't it? Do you think he's using me just so I'll make some potions for him? He really seems to like me, though. I don't think so. I think we'll be together forever.

I don't care if my dad doesn't like him. My dad doesn't have to be married to him. I know I'm young, and it's too soon to think of marriage, but it's inevitable. I can feel it. We're going to be together forever and ever. I'd do anything for him. Anything he asked of me. He's got a very promising future. I mean, he's here on a quest. I wouldn't marry a man who didn't have a quest. It shows ambition. Plus, a golden fleece—don't you want to see it? I do. I keep imagining me and Jason and the golden fleece sitting in front of a fire in our beautiful house— Oh, I'm so in love I could just die!

HELP

Someone will come for me. My mother will come for me. She will! If she doesn't, she'll find someone who will. She's not going to let me rot down here.

I wish I hadn't wandered off on my own. Why did you bring me here anyway? I don't want to be here. I want to go home!

I'll be queen? Really. Well, I don't know if I want to be queen of the Underworld. It's ugly here. And I want to see my mother!

YOU'VE GOT TO BE KIDDING

You want me to what? Cut off his hair? I'm not a hairdresser. I've never cut a man's hair in my life.

Wait a sec. Let me get this straight. His strength comes from his hair? It just seems to me like his strength might be in his muscles. I'm not a doctor or anything, but that makes sense to me.

Plus, if you can't defeat him because he's too strong, how am I supposed to do it? I'm just one girl. Why don't you do it if it's so easy? Seems to me that you're asking a girl to do what a whole army can't. I don't see any reason why I should do this. Do it yourself if it's such a good idea.

ANSWERS

SWEET, *Dairy Queen*
BAKING, *Hades*
BIG AND PROUD, *Fat Albert*
DESTINY, *Santa Claus*
JOB HAZARDS, *The Tooth Fairy*
ARACHNIPHOBIA, *Peter Parker*
I RULE, *Burger King*
OBSESSIVE, *Mr. Clean*
MY QUEST, *Medea*
HELP, *Persephone*
YOU'VE GOT TO BE KIDDING, *Delilah*

Icons of Literature, Art, and Fashion

• • •

Mary Shelley
Agatha Christie
Victor Frankenstein
Lady Macbeth
Coco Chanel
James Bond
George Sand
Robin Hood
Emily Dickinson
Georgia O'Keefe
Stephen King
Claude Monet

The Wicked Witch of the West
Hamlet
Davy Crockett
Queequeg
Whistler's Mother
Sherlock Holmes
Dracula
Pablo Picasso
William Shakespeare
Minerva McGonagall

SOLITARY

I'm nobody. Who are you? Are you nobody, too? Well, I just ask because you're eating alone. I didn't mean anything by it. You're new. Oh, well. I'm Emily. I've lived here forever. Maybe I could help you out—

Um, no. I'm not popular. I'm kinda quiet. It was actually really hard for me to come over here and talk to you. I don't usually do things like—

I'm talking too much. Sorry. I don't usually—

I'm cramping your style. Oh. Sorry. I just thought since you were eating alone and I was—Well, two is better than one, right?

Oh. OK. Sorry. I'll go now.

DIFFERENT

It's not easy being green. Going to this school puts me in such a bad mood. Everyone makes fun of me—the color of my skin, my wart, my laugh. My clothes aren't pretty and fashionable. They say only hicks come from out West.

I only have you, monkeys. You're my only friends.

How can they complain when I make their hair fall out after they call me names? I'm practicing. Doing my homework. They deserve it, those prissy witches from the east. I hate them.

I wish you could fly, monkeys, so we could get away from this place. Boarding school stinks. Why did my parents send my sister to a different school? Life is so bleak and dreary.

Monkeys, I'm going to find a way to make you fly. Would you like that? Would you be my best friends forever then?

DOUBLE O NOTHING

Well, hello. I'm *(insert last name of character), (insert full name of character)*. *(Beat.)* Yes, well, my mum couldn't come to Parent's Day 'cause she's traveling in Italy, and my dad is with the headmaster? I think they went to university together, Miss? So, no one's here to talk to my teachers but me. So, if you want to tell me about my academic performance, I'll be glad to pass on the information. *(Beat.)* No, I've done this before. It's on the up-and-up. I will tell them, Miss. I'm very trustworthy.

Yeah, well, I do keep to myself a bit. I like to watch other people. You see lots of things. For example, I know who blew the curve on your last test by cheating. *(Beat.)* I could tell you, Miss, but I don't think that's wise. *(Beat.)* Because I need to protect myself? And there is some benefit to having information people want to know. *(Beat.)* No, not blackmail, exactly. But if I should find myself in a bad situation, I can call on those individuals to help me out. It's diplomacy, Miss. *(Beat.)* No, I don't think I'll go into politics, with all due respect. I'm thinking I'll be a librarian. Or an English teacher. *(Leans in slowly.)* Like you, Miss.

MY WAY

Mom, when I said I wanted flowers on my wall, that's not quite what I meant. Well, these flowers are so . . . girlie. No, flowers don't have to be so precious and cute. Flowers are big and vibrant and colorful—No, you just don't get it! I'll show you. Can I paint my room? Myself? I just need a blank wall and some bright colors like reds and yellows and purples. I can see what I want in my head. Please, Mom. Let me do it!

Aw, I know you worked hard to put up the wallpaper. I'm sorry. I thought you understood. But this isn't what I want! It's not what I meant! I hate it! This isn't fair. It's my room.

THE SMARTASS OF STRATFORD

Milksop! Codpiece! If you come near me again, I'll festoon your pate with a cacophony of blows! Which will improve your looks, you son of a dog-faced strumpet!

What? What are you staring at? Never heard someone create language before? Is my massive intellect making you feel miniscule? Laugh if you will; if I be Will I do not mind.

No, calling me Shakesqueer is not creating language, you carbuncled dolt. Why am I cursed with such putrescence all about me? Woe is me, for all the world is filled with mediocrity. But I refuse to let it get me down into the bowels of Hades. I shall overcome even the harshest of thrashings and the mightiest of Nelsons. You may have the advantage of brute force, but I have a cranium chock-full of imaginings. You laugh now, but I will come out on the apex in the finale, minion. You will beg, sloven—I was kidding! Kidding! *(Grabbing nose.)* No! Refrain from rearranging my noble beak!

Help! Help, good people of Stratford! *(Running away.)*

JUMP-START

Here. I can fix that. Oh, sorry. I broke it. I can fix it! Honest. The other day I brought a frog back to life with my dad's jumper cables— *(Beat.)* No, I did! I'm going to figure out how to bring people back to life. *(Beat.)* I am! *(Beat.)* How? I don't know yet. Maybe I'll get some dead people from the graveyard— *(Beat.)* Well, if they died 'cause their heart didn't work, I'll get another heart. *(Beat.)* So? If they died 'cause their brain didn't work, I'll get another brain. *(Beat.)* Don't you get it? If they died 'cause they don't have legs, I'll get other legs. *(Beat.)* It doesn't matter if I find ones the same size. They'll be so happy they're alive again; it won't matter. I'll be famous. *(Beat.)* Shut up. When you die, I'm going to give you old lady legs, and I won't need to replace your brain 'cause you don't have one.

OBSERVATIONS IN SUBURBAN MAINE

I think my father is a killer. I'm serious. I saw him digging yesterday. He was probably burying a dead body in our backyard. No, I didn't see the dead body.

I am not imagining things! Well, yeah, I thought my granddad was a vampire last week. I still think he is. I know my mother said he was drinking tomato juice, but—yuck! Who drinks tomato juice? It was blood.

I found a bone behind the school the other day. Near the cafeteria garbage cans. Do you think this school could be on an Indian burial ground? I'm telling you, Charlie, strange things are going on in this town.

AMBITION

I'm going to be queen. I am! It's possible. Why not? I can just destroy everyone who stands in my way. Why do I have to get married? But I don't want to get married. Boys are pointless. I don't want to have babies! Women die having babies. I'm going to live forever. I was born to rule. Look at me! Don't I look like it? The way I stand, the way I speak—it's my destiny. I can see the crown on my head . . . throngs of people listening to my every word . . . throwing lavish dinner parties with all the best people . . . But if I have to get married to do it . . .

Well, I'll just— Can I move somewhere else and be queen? Maybe I could go to a desert island and be adored by natives! No? Then I'll—I'll—become a pirate queen. You don't need to marry anyone for that or be born into the right family. You just TAKE OVER. So that's what I'll do. Just try to stop me.

ESCAPE FROM ROKOVOKO

Father, I want to see the world. I want to see these Christians. Perhaps there is something to what they teach? How can we know if we do not listen? I'm not saying I will become one of them. I love our people and our way of life. But—does this make sense?—seeing the world will let me see for myself if this is the life I want. It could make me a better leader. For all we know, we will have to deal with these white men, these Christians, these Quakers one day on our shores. If I know how to deal with them, how to conquer them, whether they taste good with yams—

I don't deny that they may be our enemies. But I am not afraid. I am strong and tall. No man or beast will break me. My will is strong. Let me go. I will return.

MY WICKED STEPMOTHER

I hate you! How dare you read my diary! It's mine. You're jealous of me. It's pathetic. Father loves me more than you because I remind him of my mother. She was intelligent and refined and beautiful. You are an ugly old witch. Of course, visitors to the house want to talk to me, not you. You want to make me Cinderella, doing chores around the house while you, the wicked witch, indulge your precious daughter, but I won't play along. You can't make me.

Father will take my side, you'll see. He won't send me away to Scotland. You're lying!

You wouldn't do that to me, would you, Dad? I know we fight, but I want to stay here with you. Make her go away. You're my family. Dad?

How could you do this to me?

NEARSIGHTED

Do I have to go on the field trip? We're going to the country to draw pictures and have a picnic. You know my allergies bother me when I'm around all those flowers. I can't even see straight. I'm likely to walk into a tree.

I'm not exaggerating! I sneeze like crazy, my eyes water, and everything goes all smeary. Can't I stay home? I'll go down to the lake, and I'll draw that instead. There are reeds and water lilies in there; it's almost like drawing flowers, right?

MYSTERY SOLVED

I know who did it. Why, it's perfectly obvious, that's how I know. All you have to do, Molly, is keep your eyes open. Look about you. Clues are everywhere. It's a matter of paying attention to the details. And knowing a bit about human nature.

Who has the most to lose from breaking the vase? You? No. While you are certainly low on the social scale, my mother has long since gotten used to you knocking things over. Keep thinking, Molly. Who has the most to lose?

Me? Don't be silly. How could you—OK. It was me. And if you tell my mother, I'll tell her you did it!

RESISTANCE

I don't want to go to boarding school. Why should I? It won't make me a better person. I know it won't! Why can't I stay here with you and Mom? I promise I'll read every book in the library. I'll study every day. You'll be proud of me. I'll be the smartest kid in Denmark.

Please, Mom, don't make me go! I won't make any friends. The other kids won't like me. I bet I'm already smarter than all the other kids. Probably the teacher, too! Just homeschool me. I don't want to go to a place where I won't know anyone.

Horatio's going, too? The same school? Are you sure? Well, I guess I could go. I could just go see what it's like. But if it's not for me, can I come home?

NOT A MUSICIAN

No, I don't want to. I've changed my mind. I don't like to perform. I like to play. It's different. I don't like people to watch. I'd rather go to my room. I'm at a critical point in a book I'm reading. The crime is about to be solved. Personally, I think it was the victim's sister. You see—

I'll never be a pianist. I'm happy to go to lessons and play, but please don't make me do it in front of everyone. I'm sure to be a disaster. Just thinking about it makes me feel queasy.

I probably am the only girl in the world who wants to be sent to her room all the time. So I'll probably never have fans and no one will ever know who I am, but I don't mind. I'd rather think than be the center of the party.

A THIEF IS BORN

Boy, do you smell! You should consider taking a bath every once in a while. What do you mean you can't? Find some water and get in it. If you're so poor, how come you're not skinny? Shouldn't you be hungry, Johnnie?

OK, I promise. Tell me your secret. I swear I won't tell! Come on. Just tell me. You steal?! Fine, fine, I'll keep it down. I've just never met a thief before. So can you just take things without people even knowing it? Right out of their pockets? Teach me how!

I know I don't need anything. Tell you what, if you teach me, I promise I'll give what I steal to a poor person. I swear. Come on, Johnnie!

VLAD TO THE BONE

Come to me. *(Beat.)* Yes, you. I said, "Come to me!" in a creepy, commanding tone. *(Beat.)* What do you mean why? Because I told you to. I have possession of your soul. Look deep into my eyes. You are imprisoned by me. You cannot look away. *(Beat.)* I said, "You cannot look away." That guy is not hot. That is my servant. He eats bugs. Surely you cannot be imprisoned by this sorry creature of the night. It defies logic. *(Beat.)* I do not use too much gel. I am debonair.

This look is timeless. Ageless. Like me. I don't need to don the attire of your time. *(Beat.)* "It would help?" How dare you speak so to me! No, I don't drive. I fly. Oh, I give up. *(Beat.)* Do you think I have a shot with that girl over there? The shorter one with the pink shirt. *(Beat.)* No? Don't tempt me to take your soul. I could, if I wanted to.

KING OF THE WILD FRONTIER

Yeah, I killed that bear. And that moose. I killed all the deer in here, too. Why are you crying? 'Cause you're impressed? Whaddya mean, you're sad? About what? The animals? Why? They're dead. I killed 'em myself! Bang! Right between the eyes!

You're not making any sense. Hunting is fun! The animals don't mind. They don't think. They're not sad. It's survival of the fittest! I'm proud of what I did. You're bumming me out. If you're going to cry, you can just get lost.

SERIOUSLY CUTE

I can't stand being so cute and cuddly. Everyone's always patting me on the head and asking me to transfigure. What if I don't want to? Sometimes I feel like I'm in the circus. Always having to perform. Sometimes I wish my other form were a python or a hedgehog—something prickly or slimy. Please, God, please, make me less adorable. After all, I am nearly a teenager. I don't want to be thought of as a child any more.

Well, now, I suppose I'm done complaining. You ought to get working on your homework! Don't expect me to do it for you at breakfast. I would like to be able to enjoy my meal like a normal person for once!

REBEL, REBEL

Enough! No more! Stop pulling, Marie. I can't breathe. This is torture. Who ever thought this was a good idea? If I were meant to have a sixteen-inch waist, I would have been born with one. You know what I mean! It's painful and unnatural. I'm tired of having my insides tortured and squeezed each and every day. I simply won't do it anymore. There's nothing you can do to change my mind. I'm too big for you to force me into a corset and dress.

I'm going to wear boys' clothes from now on. Either that or I won't wear anything at all. I mean it. You know I'll do it. Don't test me. You'll be sorry. I'm not afraid to follow through with this.

THE UNIFORM

Mother, I am not wearing that uniform. It's plaid. Well, plaid is simply not chic! It's . . . ordinary. Entirely ordinary! It looks like a tablecloth. I don't care if the other kids wear it.

I'll make my own uniform. I know exactly what I want. All I need is the fabric. Black. Black is chic, Mother! It is not gloomy. I know I am still a girl and no one has died, but I want a simple, black dress, Mother. Then I'll make a little boxy jacket to go over it with buttons— Why can't you do this for me? Trust me. I know what I'm saying! With your pearls—

I don't want to go to that school then, Mommy. I will be so humiliated! Why are you doing this to me?

PERSPECTIVE

That is a drawing of my friend Giuseppe. What's wrong with it? He broke his nose last week in a fight. That's how he looks. How do you know he doesn't? This guy who hit him said he was going to rearrange his face, and that's just what he did. I drew this as a public record. Giuseppe is going to sue the guy who beat him up. He used to be good-looking. Now, well, he looks like this picture. That's the honest truth! Really!

I am so sick of everyone saying that I can't draw. I kinda like this picture! Why should I draw things like everyone else? Isn't art supposed to be creative?

I don't know. Maybe I just don't know what's good.

THE GOOD FRIEND

Oh, Julia. What are you wearing? That shade of gray is especially bright. It is much safer, you know, to wear a shade just the smallest bit lighter than black. Not funereal, but sensible. I'm only saying this to help you. My mother bought me the plainest bonnet yesterday. I'm so thrilled with it. I do believe that one looks best in the simplest things. Modesty is a girl's best friend. That's what I always say.

Is something wrong with your eyes, Julia? Are you about to faint? You frightened me for a moment! Your eyes were rolling about in your head! I thought for a minute that the devil had entered your very soul. Don't you ever scare me like that again! Do be sure to wear a dress closer to black tomorrow. I tell you, that shade of gray is tempting Lucifer himself.

ANSWERS

SOLITARY, *Emily Dickinson*
DIFFERENT, *The Wicked Witch of the West*
DOUBLE O NOTHING, *James Bond*
MY WAY, *Georgia O'Keefe*
THE SMARTASS OF STRATFORD, *William Shakespeare*
JUMP-START, *Victor Frankenstein*
OBSERVATIONS IN SUBURBAN MAINE, *Stephen King*
AMBITION, *Lady Macbeth*
ESCAPE FROM ROKOVOKO, *Queequeg*
MY WICKED STEPMOTHER, *Mary Shelley*
NEARSIGHTED, *Claude Monet*
MYSTERY SOLVED, *Sherlock Holmes*
RESISTANCE, *Hamlet*
NOT A MUSICIAN, *Agatha Christie*
A THIEF IS BORN, *Robin Hood*
VLAD TO THE BONE, *Dracula*
KING OF THE WILD FRONTIER, *Davy Crockett*
SERIOUSLY CUTE, *Minerva McGonagall*
REBEL, REBEL, *George Sand*
THE UNIFORM, *Coco Chanel*
PERSPECTIVE, *Pablo Picasso*
THE GOOD FRIEND, *Whistler's Mother*

Stars of TV, Film, and Music

• • •

Marilyn Monroe
Simon Cowell
Ginger Rogers
Mister Rogers
Prince
Marlon Brando
Steven Spielberg
Zsa Zsa Gabor
Laurence Olivier
Mae West
Mick Jagger
Sylvester Stallone
Dolly Parton
Liz Taylor

A STAR IS (NEARLY) BORN

I can't help it, Mama. Is it so distracting? I could stop, but I just don't wanna! When I see those girls out there dancing and singing, it's all I can do not to just jump in the middle of it! I'm actually holding myself back, doing the numbers out here in the wings. You have no idea how good I'm being! I'm not hurting anyone.

What's that thing that people say about copying—oh, I remember! "Imitation is the sincerest form of flattery." I just want to be like those girls onstage! You can understand that, can't you? You love the theater, too! I've just got to get my practice in. I have to be ready for that day, that moment, when destiny arrives. Hollywood here I come! Momma, I gotta dance or . . . well, I just gotta!

DESTROYED

Mom, Frank hit me in the face. I'm serious. I think my teeth are loose. Now I can't talk good. My voice, my beautiful voice! I sound like a mobster. It's not fair. I'll never get to sing in the boy choir like I wanted to. I'll never get to perform *Hamlet* at the Royal Shakespeare Company. What's left for me? Now I'm just a regular guy.

I need to learn how to fight. All the kids at school are going to beat me up and make fun of me. I'll get in trouble in class for mumbling. Yo, Mom, are you going to punish Frank for ruining my life or what?

FLIRT

Boys have cooties? Well, that would explain them crawling all over me. What can I say; I have a gift.

You think it's a curse? To each her own, sister. I could never understand those girls who would run from the boys on the playground. I always let 'em catch me. I'd rather be kissed than run a mile. I just wish Billy Underwood would come after me. Yesterday I asked him if he'd like to meet me under the boardwalk, and he said, "I'm working on my suntan." Can you believe it? What can I do to make him get it? I'd consider drawing him a picture, but I'm better at the art of love than the art of . . . you know, art!

Hey, Billy, come up and see me sometime! I live on the third floor! That boy will be the death of me.

BACK-LOT BACKYARD

That's not right. You have to get the timing. When you get hit by the asteroid you have to react right afterward, not ten seconds later. Or it doesn't look real. I know it's just a garbage can. You have to use your imagination, Jeff.

This isn't dumb. This is awesome! Where are you going? I know it's hot, but . . . You're coming back, right? Actors. Geez, Louise, it's always something with actors. Hey, uh, while we're waiting, let's do a retake on the chase scene, Amy, I think you can scream with a little more passion. Intensity. That's what I need. I want to see fear on your face. No, you don't need makeup. I like the sweat. The sweat is good. Makes it realistic.

Where are you going now? You're thirsty, too? Man, I have got to get some union actors in here. You guys have no work ethic!

REVOLUTION

Look guys, can we talk? What we've been doing with the band is OK. But I think we can put it over the top. You know, create a new sound. A little funk, a little Hendrix . . . And here's the main thing. I think I should sing. We need a singer. Just playing instruments—well, is that what you hear on the radio? Is that what people book in clubs? No, if you want to be really big, you need a singer. I can do it! I'll still play guitar and keyboards, that's no problem.

I can do it all. I mean it. I have a vision for this band.

This isn't an ego trip! We can really go places. Do you trust me?

CHICKEN DANCE

I was not looking at myself in the mirror. I was dancing in front of the mirror. I think I've got something here. Check out this move! Don't laugh! I've got something here.

I do not look like a chicken! I've been practicing. The problem with all the other guys is they don't pick up their feet enough. Dancing is like quick walking. And you move your arms around a bit and flick your head. Stop saying I look like a chicken! You're jealous.

Think whatever you want. I think I've got something here.

HURRAY FOR HOLLYGROVE (ORPHANS' HOME)

Do you think I'm pretty? I don't know. Sometimes I think so, and other days I think that if I were prettier, I wouldn't have to live here. There's got to be something wrong with me. No one wants to keep me.

Are you an orphan? I'm not. My momma just can't keep me. I was living with my auntie Grace for a while—she's not really my aunt—but she got married. So here I am!

Well, you're a sweet boy to say such nice things to me. I'm sure you'll be adopted by a nice family and live happily ever after! Sure, I believe that. Why not?

ALAS, THE RAIN!

Ah, how deeply I grieve for the sun, shut away from view, obscured from life. It makes we weep to think of all the rugby players, be-uniformed, sitting in a dim, bleak locker room, all games cancelled. Rain, I curse you!

Dramatic? Me? Why do you say that? Am I not a reflection of how you are feeling as well? I suppose I could put a cork in it. It's just that there's nothing else to do but moan on boring days like this.

Perhaps we could put on a play! This is perfect weather for "The Scottish Play"! *(Sighs dramatically.)* Fine. Consider me corked.

NEW VIEW

Well, darn it, if I could be flat chested, I would be. I meant it, Willadeene. It would be a mighty relief. I can't fit in my clothes! And I can't ever run. It's not easy being different than everyone else. I finally know what it must be like for people of other races and cultures. People stare at you and call you names when you're different. It's not comfortable. In fact, it's pretty gosh darn awful!

My whole world perspective has changed. I'm not kiddin'! Adversity does make you a better person, just like Jesus says. I don't mean to say I'm worse off than anyone else, but I feel for people more than I ever did before. This puts me in mind to write a song. I'll call it "The Full-Figured Blues."

CRITICAL

Wretched. Just awful. You do realize that you're supposed to actually kick the ball into the goal, don't you? You didn't even come close. You're an embarrassment.

I know I'm sitting on the bench. What's your point? I'm not blind. I can still see what a bad player you are. Look, I'm just giving you some constructive criticism. You stink like poop. If I were you, I'd be humiliated over that performance. That's all I'm saying.

Me? Go into the game? Well, I could. Look, I think you're missing the point here. I'm not saying I'm the best player that ever lived; I'm just saying that you're the worst. That's all.

A LITTLE SNAG

I got it! Oh, I knew it! I mean, I didn't know, but I had this feeling! Me. In a movie! Of course, I've done others, but this one is going to be bigger, isn't it? And I'll get to play such a heroic girl. Such a brave, strong, horse-riding girl . . .

About that horse riding, there's just one little problem. I don't really know how. And I'm a little, teensy-weensy bit scared. I'm sure I can do it, though! I learn things very quickly, you'll see! I think horses are beautiful, and I want more than anything to be in this movie.

If I can just take a few lessons before filming starts, I promise you I'll be really good, and I won't scream bloody murder even once! I'll be so brave. You'll see! You won't be sorry.

GOING OUT

(Talking slowly and gently.) I'm hurrying. Just need to button my sweater one . . . button . . . at a time. Know what? I like to take my time.

No, don't go without me. You are my friend. And I like you.

OK, I'm just . . . about . . . ready. Just need to put on my tennis shoes. Wait! Here's the mailman. Hey, Mister Mailman, is it a beautiful day in the neighborhood? *(Out straight to the audience.)* That's just terrific, isn't it, kids?

Well, I'm talking to these kids out here, Henrietta. There aren't any kids watching me? Are you sure?

CENTER OF ATTENTION

Vhat do I do? Vhat don't I do, dahlink? I am a beezy girl. Why it takes me three hours to make my hair zhis gorgeous, dahlink. Do you think I wake up like zhis? Just look at poor Eva. She only takes one hour on her hair, and it looks like a goulash.

Homevurk? Please, dahlink, you make me laugh. Homevurk is for boring girls.

Shut up! *(Mimes slapping someone.)* Was zhat boring? See, I told you. I am a fascinating voomun.

I DON'T THINK SO

So this prince, he's in love with this chick? And she's dead. And he wants to kiss her? That just doesn't seem real. I can't imagine that there would be a chick so hot that I'd want to kiss her when she's dead. And there is a bunch of little people hanging around. No, this seems weird. I can't do it. I know it's in the script, but the script don't make no sense. Now if the guy comes and sees this dead hot chick, he's going to be, like, "Ew, now that is a shame." But he ain't gonna kiss her. And with these dwarfs around, he's gonna be, like, "Excuse me, dorks, don't you have somewhere else to be? What are you pervs doing hanging around some dead girl?" Then maybe he'd slug one or two of them.

Yeah, well, I think you are gonna have to count me out of this whole Snow White thing. I gotta keep it real.

ANSWERS

A STAR IS (NEARLY) BORN, *Ginger Rogers*
DESTROYED, *Sylvester Stallone*
FLIRT, *Mae West*
BACK-LOT BACKYARD, *Steven Spielberg*
REVOLUTION, *Prince*
CHICKEN DANCE, *Mick Jagger*
HURRAY FOR HOLLYGROVE
   (ORPHANS' HOME), *Marilyn Monroe*
ALAS THE RAIN, *Laurence Olivier*
NEW VIEW, *Dolly Parton*
CRITICAL, *Simon Cowell*
A LITTLE SNAG, *Liz Taylor*
GOING OUT, *Mister Rogers*
CENTER OF ATTENTION, *Zsa Zsa Gabor*
I DON'T THINK SO, *Marlon Brando*

World Leaders

• • •

Nero
Henry VIII
Mary I of England
Elizabeth I
Tsar Ivan IV
Napoleon
Marie Antoinette
Imelda Marcos
Katherine Howard
Fidel Castro
Boudica
Cleopatra
Mahatma Gandhi
Genghis Khan
Sigrid the Haughty
Hannibal
Joseph Stalin

FRENCH SMALL FRY

I'm the boss of you and I'm the boss of you and I'm the boss of you and—

Don't interrupt!

I'm the boss of you. You, too.

Never call me shrimp. I am the boss of you! Did you forget? There will be desserts and chairs named after me! *(Insert correct name here)*! Leader! Ruler! King! Emperor! Where are you going? *(Beat.)* Russia? I'm coming too! Wait for me! I love cold weather! Hold on, guys! I'm coming with you.

Don't leave me here. I'm scared of the dark . . .

NICKNAME CALLING

Why do I have to be "the Terrible"? You get to be "the Great" and I get to be "the Terrible"? What did I do that's so terrible? And what did you do that's so great? I want to be "Ivan the Fantastic-Stupendous-Master-Meister" or "P. Diddy." One of those.

Why not? Can't I pick my own name for the rest of history if you can? Hardly seems fair. You know, Catherine is calling herself "the Great," too. She is. Are you sure you didn't copy her? Maybe we should call her "Catherine the Stink" instead. That will drive her up a wall. Louis-Philippe wants a nickname, too, but I told him his first name was too long, and there was no way to add to it.

Hey, want to pillage tomorrow? Or take over another country? Asia is huge and up for grabs. *(Beat.)* So what if it's mostly ice? *(Beat.)* Persia? That's a rug, a cat—who cares about Persia? Whatever. You can go if you want, I'm going to stay here and have a sno-cone in Siberia.

E-GYPPED

Grapes—did that. Slaves fanning me with palm fronds—check. There's nothing to do. And it's so hot. A queen's life is so limited. I see all the same people; do all the same things. It's either grown-ups, boring advisors, or slaves. And I'm not supposed to talk to the servants. I listen in on their conversations, though. What's a "brat"? I bet they mean that I'm beautiful. That's what everyone tells me.

The Romans are coming again today. They are so loud. Everything's "ciao, bella" this and "ciao, bella" that. For them, being in Egypt is a vacation, a carnival cruise around the Nile. Wonder what Rome is like. They tell me it's beautiful with huge statues, blah-blah-blah. If it's so great, how come they come here? But I'll get to dress up, so who cares?

Bring me my big headdress, slave. No, not that one. The BIG one.

GIRL WARRIOR

Get over here, boy. Did you insult that girl? Say you're sorry.

I can't make you? Are you sure about that? You don't scare me. I see you for what you are—a little boy. Picking on a girl? You should be ashamed of yourself. Where do you live?

Well, start walking. We're going to your house. We're going to tell your mother what you did. Either that, or I burn your house down while you're asleep. You think I'm kidding?

Ran away. Coward!

See, Astrid, boys are nothing to be afraid of. Next time, stand your ground and don't let any boy intimidate you. I won't ever let anyone be the boss of me. I swear it.

THE PROMISE

I promise you that I will never let the Romans come here, Dad. I swear it. In fact, I will ride up to their gates on an elephant and command them to give up. I will take over Rome. They will be so scared of me, they will tell their children, "Do you hear that? Elephant hooves! He's coming!" and all the children will run and hide. I will be a threat. You can depend on it.

Please let me ride with you today. I'll make you proud of me. If you just give me a chance, I know I can be helpful to you. For example, we'll hit less traffic if we go around the market.

Just trying to help!

TAKEOVER

Have the slaves stoke the fire. I do love a good fire. It's so beautiful. I can't keep my eyes off of it. Light some candles, too. I want to see a flame everywhere I look.

Yes, I've been practicing my speech for the senate. Don't nag. When I'm emperor, I'm going to make it a law that you can't always be telling me what to do. I'm not being a baby!

You are really cramping my style. I know you're trying to help, but I'm old enough to start making my own decisions. I hope you take care of Claudius soon. I'm ready to take over.

TEEN QUEEN

I don't like this place. It is too plain. It needs more gold. Do you think this dress is pretty? It's not. It's old. I got it a week ago. I will never wear it again.

I wish I could wear pure gold. I love it. So shiny. It always looks new. I wish I could bathe in gold. I wish I could eat gold! I do! Cake? Poo. Who wants cake? Let the poor people eat cake. I will eat gold and my insides will be shiny and I will live forever. I will! You wait and see.

PLAYER

Hi, Emily. Hey, Jane, what's up? Looking good, Agnes!

Oh, man, I love girls. I love how they giggle when I talk to them. There's nothing I love more than making a girl's face turn pink. It's a total high.

Oh, God. Here comes Helena. I'm so over her. Sure, I liked her last week, but she got so needy. "Henry, let's walk through the garden." "Henry, get the musicians to sing me a song." What about me? What if I don't want to pick roses and read poetry? I have got to shake that chick loose. Here she comes.

Helena! Stay away from me! I have a cold today, and it's all your fault. You sneezed on me. I remember. I'm serious. Don't get near me.

Come on, James, let's go find Agnes. She's so hot.

RESPECT

I can hardly be blamed for my temper. It's inherited. Maybe you don't know who my father is. If you did, perhaps you'd try to behave a little bit better in my presence. Then I wouldn't need to get angry.

My father is the king. He is! How do you know he's not? I'm not a silly girl. I'm a very smart girl. Shows what you know. You're ignorant, do you know that? See, you don't even know what ignorant means.

Girls are supposed to be smart! Only a very stupid, ignorant person would say something like that. Never mind—let's stop fighting. I think we should be friends. I like your face, Dudley.

MURDERER

Bekhter is dead. We were hunting. I'm sorry. He wanted what was mine. He was stealing from me. I hunted the animals down. He wanted to take credit. And he wanted more than was his share. He wanted to take food from our mouths.

He wouldn't listen to me! So I had to hunt him down. Besides, he's only my half-brother. He's not my real brother. He's not your son. He had no right to speak to me the way he did. He thought just because he's older—

But I'm older now. And things are going to change for the better now. You'll see. You won't miss him. I promise.

INSECURE

Would you— Can I— You're carrying a lot of books. Would you— Can I help you carry them? I mean, I'm just trying to help. If you don't want help, that's your problem. I don't care. I'm just saying, if you want help, I could help you. Carry those books. If you want.

I . . . I've seen you in school. Why are you looking at me like that? Is it my accent? The other kids don't know anything. Snobs. I have top marks, you know. I could help you with your homework. If I wanted to.

Why are you looking at me like that? Is it my face? I was sick, OK? When I was little? It's not something I can help. Know what? You can carry your own books. You're a big snob just like the others. Don't ever talk to me again.

THE STANDOFF

For the last time, Sanjay, I don't want to fight you. So hurry up and punch my face and take my lunch. Aren't you getting bored of this yet?

No, I'm not going to struggle or fight back. I still get punched. So just do it and get it over with. Go on.

Huh. Did you see that? Sanjay didn't punch me in the gut. Why do you think that is? Maybe I'm onto something here. If I ask him to punch me every day, he won't. Is that what made the difference?

This will be the first day in six years that I'll get to eat my lunch! Boy, am I hungry!

THE OTHER DAUGHTER

I have to wait on Lizzie? That's not fair. It's not right! I'm older than her. She should wait on me. Father married my mother first. I don't understand any of this. One day I'm a princess, and now I'm nothing. "Lady Mary." I don't want to be just Lady Mary. And I certainly don't want to be my little sister's slave. I want to see my mother.

(Mimes being slapped.) Ow! You hit me! How dare you? I want to see my mother now!

I can't? Ever? Why? I don't understand any of this.

WORN DOWN

What? You have to rent shoes? Shoes that other people have worn? Ew! Why? No, thank you. I'll just bowl in the shoes I'm wearing. I'll go barefoot then. Then I won't scratch the floors.

It's for my own safety? Are you joking? It can't be safe to wear the same shoes as thousands of other people who probably have green mold growing between their toes! You're not doing me any favors. Come on. I'm at a birthday party. My mom won't be here to pick me up for hours. You have to let me play.

Look, I don't want the shoes! I'm not wearing those shoes! I can hardly even stand wearing my own shoes more than once!

SEPARATE

No. I don't want to. Why should I have to do what I don't want to do? And I don't want to go to her birthday party. She's . . . she wears very ugly dresses. And she has a horrible laugh.

I do have strong opinions! What's wrong with that? I don't care about getting along with other people. Why should I? It doesn't bother me. I'd rather be on my own than with a bunch of people I don't like. Why do other people think it's so awful to be on your own?

If other people can't stand to be alone with themselves, why should I be expected to spend time with them? If you're unpleasant to yourself, how can you expect me to like you?

SNEAKY

No one's going to know. We'll just go out back, and no one will miss us. I've been smoking cigars since I was four. It's no big deal.

That's not true. Smoking doesn't affect me at all. I'm going to be a baseball player. I can run for days. It's not a problem. You worry too much.

And after I'm a baseball player, I'll be a coach because I like telling people what to do. I'll just sit on the sidelines, shouting out orders, smoking my cigar with a big beard. It'll be awesome.

'THE ROSE WITHOUT A THORN'

Aren't there rules about being king? Codes of conduct? Edicts of appearance? A painter came by yesterday to start on a portrait, and big Henry couldn't even put down a chicken leg long enough to get sketched. Have some pride! This is how he's going to be known for all of time!

Oh, I tried to tell him. But you know Henry; he thinks he always knows best. What if I had my portrait done with chicken grease oozing down my face? Can you imagine?

Thank God my sweet Mannox has better taste than that. Otherwise, I'd lose my mind married to that old oaf!

ANSWERS

FRENCH SMALL FRY, *Napoleon*
NICKNAME CALLING, *Tsar Ivan IV*
E-GYPPED, *Cleopatra*
GIRL WARRIOR, *Boudica*
THE PROMISE, *Hannibal*
TAKEOVER, *Nero*
TEEN QUEEN, *Marie Antoinette*
PLAYER, *Henry VIII*
RESPECT, *Elizabeth I*
MURDERER, *Genghis Khan*
INSECURE, *Joseph Stalin*
THE STANDOFF, *Mahatma Gandhi*
THE OTHER DAUGHTER, *Mary I of England*
WORN DOWN, *Imelda Marcos*
SEPARATE, *Sigrid the Haughty*
SNEAKY, *Fidel Castro*
'THE ROSE WITHOUT A THORN,' *Katherine Howard*

Revolutionaries and Innovators

. . .

Charlotte Corday
Sandra Day O'Connor
Martin Luther King
Martin Luther
Bella Abzug
Rosa Parks
Crazy Horse
Emma Goldman
Harriet Tubman
Ralph Nader

TIRED

Stand up. Run around the track. Do sit-ups. Well, I am tired. And I hate gym class. I am not moving when or where I don't want to. I feel like all day long people are bossing me around and telling me what to do. Clean your room. Do your homework. Go to the store. I took care of my baby sister last night, and I was up really late. Now if I want to sit down, I will.

I'm taking a stand. And my stand is that I'm going to sit. Ma'am, I mean no disrespect, but you just gotta understand me. Today I'm sitting out.

WATCHDOG

What is that you're holding? That toy is a death trap! You could kill yourself! Give that to me.

Don't cry. I'm saving your life, silly! How the government can turn their back on the toy industry and allow them to market and distribute a product that's so clearly defective—

Really, you have to stop crying now. If you need something to do, why don't you write a letter to your congressman complaining about this? It's not my fault that you can't play with this; it's his!

You don't want to write your congressman? What is this country coming to? This apathy is inexcusable. You can't expect progress if you're not prepared to shake things up a little.

Sure, go home to your mommy. Great idea. She can help you with the letter!

FEMINIST WITH A CAPITAL F

Look, I'm a Jew and I'm a girl. Get used to it. You can call me any name you like; the facts will still be the same. And I'll still think you're an obnoxious, pig-headed jerk. No, I don't hate boys. Some of you are OK. Do I think girls are better? Well, duh. We are. Just because I have different chromosomes doesn't mean I'm weak or stupid. I'm not.

You can't make me shut up. I'm going to be class president, and you can't stop me. You can have the football team vote and the cheerleader vote. I'm not speaking for them. I'm speaking for the nerd stuffed in the locker and the girl in social studies who's afraid to raise her hand and the black kid who gets yelled at for walking down the hallway. Me and my big mouth are gonna take this school back. So just back off, little man.

THE QUESTION

Sister, is it ever right for someone to be killed for a cause? An ideal? No, not like Jesus. What I mean is . . . if a person is bad, then isn't it a good thing for the world to be rid of that person? Yes, I know "thou shalt not kill," but, Sister, if you saw the devil, wouldn't you want to kill him dead?

What have I said wrong? I was just asking a question. I am genuinely curious about the answer. It just doesn't seem so simple. Bad people are punished in Hell anyway, why shouldn't they be punished during their mortal life? I do wonder about these things. If one man's death would mean a more peaceful world, I am not sure that God would disapprove of the murderer!

Yes, Sister, I will go do sixteen Hail Marys and think about my sins.

NO MORE

How am I supposed to live through this? I don't think I can. I can't bear it. I'm not strong. Or I'm not so weak. I don't know which. Is it strong to bear hard labor and beatings? Or is it stronger to refuse to go along with what you're told?

Maybe if I had a mother near me it would be a comfort. But I feel alone. I know I have you, of course. You know what I mean. You have your own life and your own children to care for. Me, well . . . I'm glad to have you. But it's not enough.

I know there's no way out. That's the worst part of it! There just has to be another way. Freedom seems a million miles away. But there just has to be a way!

THE DREAM

Dad, does God hate black people? Seems like he does. Seems like we have to work so much harder. And most of the black people I know believe in God and go to church more than white people. So how come God doesn't reward us, too? "The meek shall inherit." Well, what if I decided not to be meek? What then? What if I decided to be proud? Would God love me any less?

I had a dream last night. I made the world a more peaceful place. Everyone got what they worked for, what they deserved. It was a good dream. I hope God will let me make it come true one day.

IN CONTROL

Dad, you're driving over the speed limit. You're five miles per hour over what's allowed. That's illegal. Those laws are there to protect the public. It is our duty to respect and uphold the laws given to us. Besides, don't you care about my welfare?

Do you want some of my Tootsie Roll?

I don't eat too much candy. It's my body. I can do what I want with it. It's my right. My teeth are perfectly fine. Dad, I'm a smart girl. I can brush my teeth without being reminded. Haven't you figured out my worldviews by now? I believe in balance and fairness. So if I tell you I'll share my Tootsie Roll with you, I'll give you half of it. And if I eat half of a Tootsie Roll, I recognize that I need to brush my teeth to balance out any negative impact on my health. You should give me a little more credit, you know.

SECOND SIGHT

I had a vision. There was thunder and a white owl. The earth was dry— I am not making this up! What do you know? It wasn't a dream. This was clearer. I could see everything.

We're in danger. People are coming to take what's ours. We have to protect our people and our land. We must be prepared. I'm going to be fine. I'll live forever—

That's what my dream says! Why don't you ever believe me, He Who Rolls His Eyes Sarcastically? Well, that ought to be your name, dummy.

PROTESTOR

Oh, God, I hate Latin. It's a dead language. I don't get it. What's the point of studying it? My dad is so pretentious. He wants me to be a lawyer. He thinks that's a big, important job. Sounds boring to me. Besides, Jesus said we should be humble. I don't need an important job.

No, I'm not gonna be a priest. I'll probably end up being a lawyer. I think—well, maybe I might want to have a family or something some day. So I'll just do what my dad says.

Oh no. Here comes You Know Who. I hate it when he calls me "God Boy." It's rude. And not true! God loves everyone, not just me. Even big, hairy, smelly kids like him.

Leave me alone or . . . or . . . you'll go to hell! I mean it!

ANSWERS

TIRED, *Rosa Parks*
WATCHDOG, *Ralph Nader*
FEMINIST WITH A CAPITAL F, *Bella Abzug*
THE QUESTION, *Charlotte Corday*
NO MORE, *Harriet Tubman*
THE DREAM, *Martin Luther King*
IN CONTROL, *Sandra Day O'Connor*
SECOND SIGHT, *Crazy Horse*
PROTESTOR, *Martin Luther*

Athletes and Adventurers

· · ·

Jack LaLaine
Mia Hamm
Amelia Earhart
Mike Tyson
Richard Simmons
Annie Oakley
Christopher Columbus
Muhammad Ali
Wilma Rudolph

YOU AIN'T MY PARTNER

Get outta my way. I'll punch your lights out, mister. You better hightail it outta here; you're makin' me mad. *(Beat.)* I may be shorter than you, but I've got more gumption and a whole lot more smarts than a chump like you. Bring it on, bubba.

(Throwing one punch. Then talking to the ground.) I may be a lotta things, but I ain't a liar; I warned you.

(Looking eye level again.) Don't ever call me "missy" or "little girl" again. I'm grown up, if you haven't noticed. I have lived life. I have seen the world. I have survivor skills. So don't be telling me I'm too little or too young to do anything. I can do anything and everything I wanna do. That includes flattening you like a weasel under a wagon wheel. And doncha forget it, mister!

FREE

God, I wish I could be a bird. Look at that blue sky. I could look at it forever. Have you ever just wanted to go? You know what I mean, just go? Not anywhere in particular. Just away. Keep moving. I'd love to go somewhere I've never been before. What do you think Madagascar is like? You know, in Africa? What would it be like to see an aardvark in person? There's so much to see in this world!

I can't wait 'til I'm older. How old do you think you need to be to just go out in the world? On days like this, sunny, beautiful days, I almost can't bear sitting still. It makes me want to scream! My heart feels like it's going to burst. I wish I could just get on the back of a bird and fly!

Race you home? *(Runs to the door.)*

MOTIVATION

What are you just lying there for? Get up! There's ten minutes of recess to go! Don't be a girlie. This is important! Where's your competitive spirit? You can't just say "I don't want to play anymore." You're in this! You're on a team. They're counting on you.

Look at me. I'm twelve, and I'm in top physical condition. But you should be in even better shape than I am! You're only ten, for Pete's sake! If you keep going on like this, you'll be a weak has-been baby by the time you're in your teens. Is that what you want? Is it? Is it?!

Hey, you can't tag me. I'm just coaching. I'm not playing.

SEA DOG

I did, too, go out at sea when I was ten! What was it like? Well, it was wet. I ate a biscuit so hard it broke six of my teeth. I did! I got scurvy. It was gross. But I'm OK now.

Yeah, I'll probably do it again. It was tough, but it was worth it. I had blisters on my hands, and my face was red from the sun, and I was tired and hungry, but there's nothing like being on a ship. Where did we go? You know, faraway lands and all that.

Well, OK, Sicily. But it took a long time to get there!

THE CHAMP

Baby, I'm the best thing on two feet. Look at my moves. Did you ever see footwork like that? Answer the question! Did you ever see footwork that smooth? So quick, so graceful, like some kind of superhero or angel or something equally superspectacular? I didn't think so. And that's just the beginning of my talent. I can philosophize, harmonize, fantasize—

No. I don't know the answer. I don't mathesize. Is it eight?

Well, if you're sure you want me to . . . I'll sit down.

FASTER

Wait! I can't believe I missed the bus. This is not a good start to the school year! If I'm late, I'll get detention. And if I get detention, I won't be able to get my homework done before my mom gets home. And if I don't get my homework done before my mom's home, I'm dead. I've either got to get up earlier in the morning or run faster after the bus. Well, there's no choice, I've got to run faster! There's no way I'm going to wake up sooner!

Come on, if we hurry up, maybe we won't be late!

CHUBBY

I am sick to death of the kids at school making fun of me. I am a human being! Why are they so cruel? I can't help that I'm chubby. I'm made that way. Our whole family is made that way.

You know what? If all the fat kids in school got together, we could take over, I bet. We could kick the butts of all those mean kids, and the school would be ours. I know, Momma. I was just . . . wishing. But you're right. You catch more flies with honey. I am going to be so friendly and sooo nice that everyone will have to like me.

Know what else? I am going to walk around this neighborhood with my head held high because I am a good person. I can do it! If I don't come back in twenty minutes, send an ambulance after me.

GO TEAM

Pass me the ball! Pass me the ball! What? Why are you calling time out? Yes, Miss Benson? I'm being a team player. I'm on the team, and I'm playing! So, yeah, I'm a team player. Did you see what was going on out there? Wendy would not pass me the ball. How are we going to win this game if she won't pass to me? I know I could have made that goal.

Sit on the bench? You're joking, right? This team will bomb without me, Miss Benson! It's suicide! I'm only thinking of the team.

I am not a ball hog, Erica! Look, I can't help it if—OK, OK! I get it, Miss Benson. Fine. I'll pass more often. I promise. Can I just get out there and play?

BIG BOY

So what? I got kicked out of junior high. Look at where we live! Does it matter if I go to school? No. It doesn't matter at all.

I'm going out. That's all you need to know. I'm going to meet some friends, OK?

I don't want to talk about what happened. It's what always happens. Some kid made fun of my voice, my lisp, and I hit him. Hit him hard. And I'm not sorry. I taught him a lesson.

No, I'm not scared of going to jail! What's the difference? Mom, don't get sad. I'll make everything all right. You see if I don't. I'm gonna come home with some money tonight. Don't worry about how. I don't want you to worry, Mom.

ANSWERS

YOU AIN'T MY PARTNER, *Annie Oakley*
FREE, *Amelia Earhart*
MOTIVATION, *Jack LaLaine*
SEA DOG, *Christopher Columbus*
THE CHAMP, *Muhammad Ali*
FASTER, *Wilma Rudolph*
CHUBBY, *Richard Simmons*
GO TEAM, *Mia Hamm*
BIG BOY, *Mike Tyson*

Presidents, Vice Presidents, and First Ladies
• • •

Dick Cheney
Dwight D. Eisenhower
Dolley Madison
Richard Nixon
Dan Quayle
Abe Lincoln
Hillary Clinton
Martha Washington

THE OTHER BOY GEORGE

He has wooden teeth? You can't make me marry him! He's a soldier. So, he's dirty. Mom! If I kiss him, I'll get splinters! It's wrong and you can't make me!

What's his name? *(Beat.)* George? That's a terrible name. George Washington. Ick. Sounds like he's a nerd. George Washington.

Dad, I don't care what you say; you can't make me marry some icky old smelly soldier who spends his life camping out in the dirt. Plus, isn't he a revolutionary? What if he's on the losing side? What then? I'll be an outcast! I'll be the wife of a traitor! No money, no friends—maybe I'd even go to jail!

Please don't make me do this. I can feel it in my bones. This George Washington is bad news.

HONEST

I am not a crook! I earned an A fair and square. Not one single time did I look at John's paper. I am innocent. Really! Why doesn't anyone believe me?

Look at my face. Am I trustworthy? Am I truthful? Yes—what do you mean no? You don't think I have an honest face? Unbelievable. Do you think I am not capable of earning an A on this test? I am an excellent student.

Well, you are just going to have to prove I cheated. Can't we just work something out? I swear I didn't do anything wrong.

NOT PLAYING

No, I don't want to play. I don't play. I sit. And I think. And I weigh things over. Leave me alone! I don't want to play with you.

Grouchy. You think I'm grouchy. Know what? I don't actually care what you think.

House. You're playing house. Like the legislative branch? Wait, you mean house like Mommy and Daddy? Ridiculous. No, I wouldn't want to play doctor instead. Tell you what. I'll play government. Come on! It'll be fun.

PARTING WAYS

Do not kill. Do not fight. Here's what I don't get, Dad. What if you had to? Like what if some guy came into the house with a gun and said he was gonna kill Mom. Would you say, "OK, if you must," or would you fight him?

What if you couldn't talk to him? The guy's crazy, Dad. Don't walk away! I'm asking you a question. It's not silly. I just don't know if I really, really understand all this Jehovah's Witness stuff. It just seems like there are times when you might have no choice. You might have to—you know.

It's possible! So then you're going to hell? So then George Washington is in hell, Dad? Cowboys are in hell?

I don't mean to make Dad mad, Milton. I just got to thinking. I want to be a soldier or a police officer. So sooner or later Dad and I are going to fight about this. I figure we may as well get it over with now.

STINKIN'

Excuse you! I am trying to get some privacy here. But I guess that's impossible. Isn't there any way in the whole universe we can get a bigger house? I'm about to hit my head on the ceiling.

I'm sorry. I'm sorry. I know we can't get another house. It's just that sometimes I wish—

But I'm being ungrateful. There are people without a home. I know that.

If it's all the same to you, Mother, I'd like to stay inside. All the kids keep saying to me, "How's the weather up there," and, well, it's not that funny a joke. Plus, I'm in the middle of a great book—

I washed up last week. Why? I know I'm growing—I really don't want to talk about this. Fine! I'll just go outside if I smell so bad!

THE HOSTESS WITH THE MOSTESS

Essie, Daddy says we're moving North soon. We're going to Philadelphia. What do you think it will be like there? Daddy says it snows there. White flakes falling from the sky. Sounds ridiculous, doesn't it? Snow? But I guess it's just like colder rain.

Oh, leave that there! We're at war, so I keep that saber by my bed in case the British attack. If they come here, Essie, I'll gut at least fifty of them! I know that's not nice, but people can't be nice during war. They have to stand and fight. Don't worry, Essie, I'll protect you.

In the meantime, let's plan a going-away party. We'll invite the nicest people! I want everyone to miss me when I'm gone!

IN CHARGE

I'm not from New York, but I tell everyone I am. It sounds tough, doesn't it? I like that. I don't want anyone to mess with me. I am a powerful woman. I want to be taken seriously. Do you take me seriously?

You should run for class president. I'll be your campaign manager. You won't have to do anything. I'll tell you what to do, what to wear, what to say. It'll be fun! What do you think?

Hey! Get your eyes off that bimbo and listen to me when I talk to you!

WINNER?

Do you think I have a chance to win the school spelling bee? I think I might. Give me some test words. "Quiet." Ummm, S-H-H-H. Is that right? No? Give me another one. Squirrel. OK. S-K-W—Wrong again? Are you sure? I think you'd better look it up. I'm pretty sure squirrel begins with S-K-W.

Oh, man, maybe I can be sick on the day of the bee. I feel sick just thinking about it now. If I can't win, I'm not sure I want to play.

You're right. I am the smartest boy in the world. I will win that bee. Thanks, Mom!

ANSWERS

THE OTHER BOY GEORGE, *Martha Washington*
HONEST, *Richard Nixon*
NOT PLAYING, *Dick Cheney*
PARTING WAYS, *Dwight D. Eisenhower*
STINKIN', *Abe Lincoln*
THE HOSTESS WITH THE MOSTESS, *Dolley Madison*
IN CHARGE, *Hillary Clinton*
WINNER?, *Dan Quayle*

Scientists, Inventors, Doctors, and Nurses
• • •

Arthur "Spud" Melin
Jane Goodall
Dr. Phil
Albert Schweitzer
Albert Einstein
Alexander Graham Bell
Marie Curie
Isaac Newton
Florence Nightingale
Ben Franklin
Whitcomb L. Judson

INVENTIVE

I made you a sled. And a chair. And scissors. I was bored. There's a lot of stuff lying around in the garage. I'm getting started on a spaceship. I'm going to make one so we can go to the moon. Why are you laughing? It's possible. I could do it. I've already made one hundred and eighty-seven things and created six brand-new inventions. No one appreciates me around here. Except maybe Mom. She likes the carving knife I made her out of—

I didn't use anything you need, Dad. Maybe just some nails. Oh, yeah. I used some wood. You needed that? But I needed it to make the chair and the sled. I can't believe I'm being sent to my room for this!

THE STRAY

Oh, Dad, can we keep him? Look, he's so cute. I promise I'll take care of him. I know I already have a pet. I want lots of pets! Animals are so sweet. Do you think we could get a monkey? Or a snake? Or both?! Please, Dad, please, let me at least keep this puppy. He'll starve if I don't take care of him. Look, he likes you!

Calm down, he's only trying to show you how much he likes you! Ranger, get off my dad's leg now! I mean it! Dad, I'll teach him not to do this; I promise! Please don't be mad and let me keep him. Ranger, down!

THE FIGHT

Look, I get that you're upset, Joey; I do. But do you really want to fight me? What are you getting out of this? Why not just hit a punching bag if you just want to unload some aggression? What do you really want?

Look, we can go through with this fight. I'm not afraid of you, Joey. I just want you to take a moment to think about this. It seems to me like you have anger issues. Have you thought about joining a sports team? Then you'd have better self-esteem. You could be part of something positive, something you could be proud of. You can't gain respect through intimidation. Trust me on this.

Look, Joey, I'll be straight with you. No one likes you. I'm giving you a chance to turn things around here. No? Not interested? OK, then. *(Pushing up his sleeves.)* Let's get ready to rumble, pal.

ONE-TRACK MIND

Nothing's wrong. Everything's fine. A noise? I didn't hear anything.

I'm pale? I'm always pale. Don't worry about me. I'm fine. I just lost track of time. I was studying. I'll go eat something now. Sometimes when I'm working on a new theory, I just forget to eat. And sleep. But after school today, I'll take a little nap.

Wait! Ummm, I wouldn't go up there if I were you. Well, something kind of exploded. I promise I'll clean it up after school. Gotta go!

SCHOOL SCHMOOL

"Wrong"! That's what he said. Very helpful. Thanks a lot! What a great learning institution school is. If you don't give a teacher the exact answer he wants, you get an F. This is why I like math! If I have to deal with these people who have no imagination, then we should only work with numbers. There, there is a right and wrong answer. It can be calculated and weighed and measured fairly. But when you write an essay that makes perfect sense about a stupid book, you fail if the teacher doesn't agree with you. Even if you prove your point! It doesn't matter.

I'm not going back there. School is for dummies. I'll just study my math books at home. In fact, I bet I'm already smart enough for college. I'm just going to go to college instead. Then I can study what I like. No more stories and foreign languages and history! Give me numbers—math and science.

I've made up my mind. I won't do anything I don't want to do ever again—no school and no hair brushing!

SHUT IT

Owie, owie, owie! *(Puts his finger in his mouth.)* I'm just trying to come up with something to replace buttons. I hate them!

Look, they're always coming undone. I'll just be sitting in school and a bunch of girls will start giggling. They don't stay shut! And then you get treated like some kind of pervert for the rest of the day. Don't even get me started on what happens if you try to button your fly again with everyone looking! I'll never try that again. The look on Miss Josephine's face! I'd rather sit there with my pants unbuttoned!

Look, there has to be a way to keep the fly of my pants shut when I want it shut, but that isn't hard to open when—well, when it needs to be opened. I thought my last experiment would work, but I closed my fingers in it, and—

I'm going to keep trying. There has to be a way!

CONSIDERATION

I can't go to bed. Marie is asleep on my arm. I don't want to wake her. If it makes you feel any better, my arm is asleep!

I know she's just a cat, but it seems unkind, don't you think? If I were sleeping peacefully, I wouldn't like it if someone woke me up by yanking the pillow out from under my head! I could just sleep here tonight. I don't mind.

It seems to me that people should be kinder to each other. To all creatures, really. We're all just trying to live in this world. If I can make one creature happy and peaceful each day, then the world will be a better place. We'd all live longer. There would be peace. I bet people wouldn't be as sick, either! *(Standing.)* Hey, I think I'm onto something!

Oh, Marie, I'm sorry! I didn't mean to! I feel terrible.

CURIOUS

How come nothing ever falls up? And, at the same time, how come if everything falls down, we can still pick our feet up and stuff? Maybe the ground affects people differently. For instance, Will says his mother never gets out of bed 'til noon every day. Maybe the time of day has something to do with it?

Then again, in summertime I feel like it's harder to move. So maybe heat has something to do with it. If the earth is round, how come no one slides down onto the South Pole if they go too far? Or maybe they have.

I've heard the South Pole is cold, like the North Pole. That doesn't make sense, does it?

I can't help talking so much. There's just so much to understand!

NOTHING TO DO

I'm tired of all the games and sports we always play. It's always the same stuff! Can't anybody come up with anything new? The whole world is boring.

I tried throwing open umbrellas—they don't go far enough. I threw forks at a pumpkin. Even when they hit, they wouldn't stick in the pumpkin. I tried throwing second graders, and I got detention. There just has to be a new game or sport that hasn't been invented. I don't want to do anything that has to do with a ball or the word *tag*.

Come on. We're going to go through the kitchen and the garage until we find something to do!

IDEA

Hey, Manny! Hey! Over here! There has to be an easier way. I'm getting hoarse yelling. I wish I could throw my voice. Wouldn't that be awesome! I could say to people on the street, "Look behind you!" and they'd turn around and no one would be there! That would be hilarious. It could have tons of uses besides practical jokes, too. Cowboys could just, say, throw their voice behind their herd of cattle to get them to come home. It could work! OK, maybe that's not a good idea. But I think everyone should learn to throw their voice. I could talk to people in China! It could work if I got really good at it.

Louis, let me get this straight. You believe that aliens are going to take over the earth, but you don't think I can throw my voice to China? That doesn't make any sense.

ROMANTIC

Oooh. Look at him. Penny, I can't help that I like guys in uniform. They just look so handsome. So bold. So proud. If I could spend all day and night around them, it would be sheer heaven!

Don't you dare tell Mom. I'll tear you limb from limb. And then we'll have to tear up your new dress to tend to your wounds. And I'll have to nurse you back to health to atone for my sins. So I'll be at your bedside all the time. Is that what you want?

Then keep your mouth closed or I'll sew it shut!

ANSWERS

INVENTIVE, *Ben Franklin*
THE STRAY, *Jane Goodall*
THE FIGHT, *Dr. Phil*
ONE-TRACK MIND, *Marie Curie*
SCHOOL SCHMOOL, *Albert Einstein*
SHUT IT, *Whitcomb L. Judson*
CONSIDERATION, *Albert Schweitzer*
CURIOUS, *Isaac Newton*
NOTHING TO DO, *Arthur "Spud" Melin*
IDEA, *Alexander Graham Bell*
ROMANTIC, *Florence Nightingale*

Spies, Informers, Reporters, Newsmakers, and Money Takers

• • •

Emma Goldman

Donald Trump

Lucretia Borgia

Mother Teresa

Emily Post

William Mark Felt Sr. ("Deep Throat")

Mata Hari

Geraldo Rivera

Helen of Troy

Madam C. J. Walker

PANTS ON FIRE

I am a princess. From the Far East. My father is hiding here. He is a spy. I know he owns the hat store. Don't you see? It's just a cover. Your dad knew my dad when he was little.

Oh, Angie, don't you have any imagination? I'm going to have to find a new best friend. You're too literal. Don't you see? All kinds of things are possible. Why do you think I have dark hair? I can sit in the sun and never burn. It's obvious that I have another mother. An exotic mother. Someday she'll return, and we'll live in a castle.

Oh, don't get me wrong. I love my mother. She is a sweet, dear creature. I love her hugely! She's been so kind to care for me all these years. Perhaps she knows I will reward her when my real mother arrives with rubies from the Indies. Won't you be jealous, Angie! Just you wait. It will happen just as I say.

EXCAVATION

We are about to discover the truth about Michael Walker, a.k.a. Mikey, and the contents of his locker. This is a moment that many have waited for: Jennifer Alvarez, who is missing her protractor; Leonard Pickle, who had his underwear stolen while in gym class; and Libby Glass, who swears her science homework disappeared from her Trapper Keeper. What other prized possessions could be in this tiny metal box? We'll find out after I take a quick bathroom break.

What? I gotta go! Besides, it's good to build suspense. This is the news story of the year. The people deserve to know the truth. That sounds good. Write that down. Hey, take a picture. I think I'm getting a mustache. See? See? Oh, forget it. Just take the picture. This is a historic moment.

OK, fine, back to the story. We are now opening Mean Mikey Walker's locker. Brace yourself. Stuff could start flying everywhere. Here we go . . . There! A shocking— It's empty. Empty! Not even a book! OK, who warned him? You guys really stink!

SELF-MADE WOMAN

Being a wife at fourteen was not what I thought it would be. I pictured myself baking pies and cuddling little babies. It's hard! It's so hard that my hair is starting to fall out! I'm worn out to pieces. I don't even feel like the same girl anymore.

I used to look in the mirror and, well—forgive me for saying this—I was pretty! Really and truly. Now . . . well, I'm not the same. Let's just leave it at that. It's not as if I've been a pampered rich girl. I've picked cotton all my life. So I'm used to work. But having to work all day and deal with a husband—well, it's too much.

Can I tell you a secret? I think there must be a better way to live. That's not the secret! The secret is . . . I know Moses isn't going to find it. It's up to me. I have to be the one to make the money and get us a better life. And I don't know how I'm gonna do it when I am so darn tired!

PROPER

No, no. My parents will be thrilled to have you to dinner tonight. Just remember to write a thank-you note once you get home. You like our house? My father is an architect. You're just going to love it here. Miss Graham's is absolutely the best school. All the finest girls go there. Where are you from again?

Detroit. Really. I've never been there. Is it . . . nice? Well, I'm sure you'll find New York exciting. We have regular balls and dinner parties. Have you ever had paté? You'll just adore it. Why, yes, it's duck's liver. On toast it's divine. Oh, you're using the wrong fork. Work from the outside in with your silverware. Um, your napkin. That should be on your lap. Yes. That way—

Oh, God. The soup. Um, never mind. It's nothing. It's just that— you must tip it away from you! AWAY! Not toward you. What did they teach you in Detroit?

THE DRINK

Drink this? Why? What if I don't want to? Why do you insist? What's in it? Suspicious? Me? Don't be ridiculous. I'm just not thirsty.

How is Gianni today? Still feeling under the weather. What a terrible shame. Perhaps it's something he ate. You can't be too careful.

That's why I don't eat or drink that I didn't have tested by servants. Just in case. Pestilence and all that. Um, excuse me. I think . . . perhaps Gianni is thirsty. I'll go make him something myself.

I know! I am such a nice girl!

WHAT A GIRL REALLY WANTS

You think this is great? Romantic? Exciting? Live my life, sister. This is terrible. Two boys fighting over me. Do they ask me what I think? No, of course not. I'm not sure I like either of them. I'm not sure either of them like me. They don't even know me. They just say I'm pretty. "Oh, Helen, you're so pretty." "Helen, your lips are like rosebuds." Rosebuds. They really do say that. See what I'm saying? It's a little icky. Plus, half the time they show up to see me with black eyes and split lips from fighting each other. Ugh! Maybe they are cute, but how would I know? I only see them when they're a wreck, all black and blue. I think they think it impresses me.

I think I'd like one nice boy who doesn't get in fights and asks me what I think about things and listens to my answers!

TOP SECRET

Psst! Over here! Don't look at me! Just listen. I've asked you to come here because I have some information. Information I think you'll find interesting. Mrs. Grouper, the health and PE teacher, smokes! I saw her sneaking a cigarette behind the gym last week. If that doesn't blow your mind, check this out: Mr. Johnson and Miss Partridge were kissing yesterday in the teacher's lounge! They're engaged? Oh. Well, how about this: All those missing books from the library? Morton Scleckel has them in his locker. He says he's doing research. Please, research? He is obviously a kleptomaniac!

Not good enough? Well . . . Margaret Yardley was late for school because she was putting on makeup in the bathroom. The captain of the football team is failing home economics. Geez—what is it going to take to get a column in the paper?

THE MISSION

What do you think it's like to be a missionary? Imagine traveling to foreign places and caring for people in the deepest, darkest, saddest places in the world. I think it sounds beautiful. I don't care if mosquitoes bite me! If it were for the greater good, I'd be bitten by thousands of mosquitoes and crocodiles besides! Have you ever heard of Bernadette, the girl who had visions of the Virgin Mary? Or Joan of Arc? I wish God would speak to me or that Mary would show herself to me. Once I thought I saw something in a tree, and I stared at it for days on end, but nothing else happened. And I could never be sure.

I just can't wait 'til I'm old enough to really see the world with my own eyes. All of it—even the worst things it has to show me.

BOSS OF YOU

Look, how can you expect to sell lemonade with such a dinky little stand? It needs to be bigger! Brighter! Right now it's not even big enough to get my hair into. You need lights. And dancing girls! Isn't there a dance school around here? People love to see pretty girls. And you have to convince people that your lemonade has something no other brand has! What's in this stuff? Water, lemons, and sugar. That's it. Well, that's not good enough! You need some razzmatazz!

Move over, kid. You don't have the stuff. I'm taking over. You're fired!

AFTER THE POGROM

I'm scared. All the windows were broken in Mr. Horowitz's store today. Every day something new is happening to the Jewish families. People are being killed! How long before it's us?

I don't want to move away. How do we know anywhere else will be better? *(Beat.)* What if we fought back? Sitting back and being invisible isn't helping. Why should we just take this? It's not fair. I saw a policeman push Adam Levin yesterday. What is it going to take for us to strike back? How many times are we supposed to take being called "dirty Jews"? I know I'm just a kid, but I want to do something. I'm tired of being quiet and ashamed.

ANSWERS

PANTS ON FIRE, *Mata Hari*
EXCAVATION, *Geraldo Rivera*
SELF-MADE WOMAN, *Madam C. J. Walker*
PROPER, *Emily Post*
THE DRINK, *Lucretia Borgia*
WHAT A GIRL REALLY WANTS, *Helen of Troy*
TOP SECRET, *William Mark Felt, Sr. ("Deep Throat")*
THE MISSION, *Mother Teresa*
BOSS OF YOU, *Donald Trump*
AFTER THE POGROM, *Emma Goldman*

Index of Names

Abzug, Bella, 78
Albert, Fat, 4
Ali, Muhammad, 92
Antoinette, Marie, 62

Bell, Alexander Graham, 119
Bond, James, 18
Boudica, 59
Brando, Marlon, 53
Burger King, 8

Castro, Fidel, 71
Chanel, Coco, 35
Cheney, Dick, 102
Christie, Agatha, 29
Claus, Santa, 5
Clean, Mr., 9
Cleopatra, 58
Clinton, Hillary, 106
Columbus, Christopher, 91
Corday, Charlotte, 79
Cowell, Simon, 49
Crazy Horse, 83
Crockett, Davy, 32
Curie, Marie, 113

Dairy Queen, 2
Delilah, 12
Dickinson, Emily, 16
Dracula, 31

Earhart, Amelia, 89
Elizabeth I, 64
Einstein, Albert, 114
Eisenhower, Dwight D., 103

Fairy, The Tooth, 6
Frankenstein, Victor, 21
Franklin, Ben, 110

Gabor, Zsa Zsa, 52
Gandhi, Mahatma, 67
Goodall, Jane, 111

Hades, 3
Hamlet, 28
Hamm, Mia, 95
Hannibal, 60
Haughty, Sigrid the, 70
Henry VIII, 63
Holmes, Sherlock, 27
Hood, Robin, 30
Horse, Crazy, 83
Howard, Katherine, 72

Ivan IV, 57

Jagger, Mick, 45
Judson, Whitcomb L., 115

Khan, Genghis, 65

King, Burger, 8
King, Martin Luther, 81
King, Stephen, 22

LaLaine, Jack, 90
Lincoln, Abe, 104
Luther, Martin, 84

Macbeth, Lady, 23
Madison, Dolley, 105
Marcos, Imelda, 69
Mary I of England, 68
McGonagall, Minerva, 33
Medea, 10
Melin, Arthur "Spud," 118
Monet, Claude, 26
Monroe, Marilyn, 46
Nader, Ralph, 77
Napoleon, 56
Nero, 61
Newton, Isaac, 117
Nightingale, Florence, 120
Nixon, Richard, 101

O'Connor, Sandra Day, 82
O'Keefe, Georgia, 19
Oakley, Annie, 88
Olivier, Laurence, 47

Parker, Peter, 7
Parks, Rosa, 76
Parton, Dolly, 48
Persephone, 11
Phil, Dr., 112
Picasso, Pablo, 36
Prince, 44

Quayle, Dan, 107
Queen, Dairy, 2
Queequeg, 24
Rogers, Ginger, 40

Rogers, Mister, 51
Rudolph, Wilma, 93

Sand, George, 34
Santa Claus, 5
Schweitzer, Albert, 116
Shakespeare, William, 20
Shelley, Mary, 25
Sigrid the Haughty, 70
Simmons, Richard, 94
Spielberg, Steven 43
Stalin, Joseph, 66
Stallone, Sylvester. 41

Taylor, Liz, 50
Tooth Fairy, the, 6
Tubman, Harriet, 80
Tudor, Elizabeth I, 64
Tudor, Henry VIII, 63
Tudor, Mary I of England, 68
Tyson, Mike, 96

Vasilyevich, Tsar Ivan IV, 57

Washington, Martha, 100
West, Mae, 42
West, The Wicked Witch of the, 17
Whistler, Anna (Whistler's Mother), 37

THE AUTHOR

KRISTEN DABROWSKI is an actress, writer, acting teacher, and director. The actor's life has taken her all over the United States and England. Her other books, published by Smith and Kraus, include *The Ultimate Monologue Book for Middle School Actors Volume I: 111 One-Minute Monologues*, *The Ultimate Audition Book for Teens Volume III: 111 One-Minute Monologues*, the *10+* play series, the *Teens Speak* series, *20 Ten-Minute Plays for Teens Volume 1,* and *111 One-Minute Monologues of Teens: Just Comedy!* Currently, she lives in the world's smallest apartment in New York City. You can contact the author at monologuemadness@yahoo.com.

THE ULTIMATE AUDITION BOOK FOR MIDDLE SCHOOL ACTORS SERIES

Volume 1: 111 One-Minute Monologues by Kristen Dabrowski

Volume 2: 111 One-Minute Monologues by Janet Milstein

Volume 3: 111 One-Minute Monologues by L. E. McCullough

THE ULTIMATE AUDITION BOOK FOR TEENS SERIES

Volume 1: 111 One-Minute Monologues by Janet Milstein

Volume 2: 111 One-Minute Monologues by L. E. McCullough

Volume 3: 111 One-Minute Monologues by Kristen Dabrowski

Volume 4: 111 One-Minute Monologues by Debbie Lamedman

Volume 5: 111 Shakespeare Monologues

Volume 6: 111 One-Minute Monologues for Teens by Teens by Debbie Lamedman

Volume 7: 111 Monologues from Classical Theater, 2 Minutes and Under by Debbie Lamedman

Volume 8: 111 Monologues from Classical Literature, 2 Minutes and Under by Debbie Lamedman

Volume 9: 111 Monologues from Contemporary Literature, 2 Minutes and Under by Debbie Lamedman

Volume 10: 111 One-Minute Monologues for Teens by Teens by Kristen Dabrowski

Volume 11: 111 One-Minute Monologues by Type by Kristen Dabrowski

Volume 12: 111 One-Minute Monologues — Just Comedy! by Kristen Dabrowski

Volume 13: 111 One-Minute Monologues — Active Voices by Marco Ramirez

I'M CONNOR THE PROFESSOR
NORFOLK PUBLIC LIBRARY